"BLACK CAT" DIVISION

17th INDIAN DIVISION

The Naval & Military Press Ltd

Published by

The Naval & Military Press Ltd
Unit 5 Riverside, Brambleside
Bellbrook Industrial Estate
Uckfield, East Sussex
TN22 1QQ England

Tel: +44 (0)1825 749494

www.naval-military-press.com

In reprinting in facsimile from the original, any imperfections are inevitably reproduced and the quality may fall short of modern type and cartographic standards.

BADGES OF CORPS AND UNITS WHICH SERVED WITH THE DIVISION

British Army

Indian Army

(Continued inside back cover.)

THE "BLACK CAT" DIVISION

An Account of the achievements
of the famous
17th INDIAN DIVISION in Burma
during the Second World War.

DIVISIONAL COMMANDERS

Maj.-Gen. D. T. Cowan, C.B., C.B.E., D.S.O., M.C., commanded 2nd March 1942 to 22rd June 1945.

Maj.-Gen. J. G. Smyth, V.C., M.C., commanded early in 1942.

Maj.-Gen. W. A. Crowther, C.B.E., D.S.O. commanded from 22nd June 1945.

The Victoria Cross

The Division has the distinction of seven of its soldiers having won the Victoria Cross.

This is the highest number of V.C.s which have been gained by any one Division during the war.

★

Here are the men who won the supreme award for gallantry.

Hav. GAJE GHALE 2/5th ROYAL GURKHA RIFLES

MAY 1943

HAVILDAR Gaje Ghale commanded a platoon of young soldiers ordered to take part in an assault on a hill which was a key position of the enemy in the Chin Hills. The approach was along a knife-edged ridge with precipitous sides and bare of cover. While preparing to attack, the platoon came under heavy mortar fire but Havildar Gaje Ghale rallied his men and led them forward. In the heavy fire which met them, Gaje Ghale was wounded in the arm, chest and leg by a grenade but, regardless of these wounds and the intense fire, he led his men to close grips with the enemy and bitter hand-to-hand fighting ensued. Covered with blood from his neglected wounds, he led assault after assault encouraging the platoon by shouting the Gurkha battle cry, "Ayo Gurkhali." Spurred on by his example, the platoon stormed and carried the hill at heavy cost to the Japanese. Havildar Gaje Ghale refused to have his wounds dressed until ordered to the regimental aid post by an officer.

Rfn GANJU LAMA, M.M.,   1/7th GURKHA RIFLES

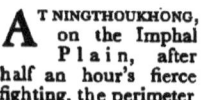

JUNE 1944

AT NINGTHOUKHONG, on the Imphal Plain, after half an hour's fierce fighting, the perimeter defences were breached at one point and Jap infantry and tanks broke through, pinning our men to the ground with intense fire. Troops ordered to counter-attack came under intense enemy tank-gun fire at point-blank range as well as from small arms. On his own initiative, Ganju Lama crawled forward and engaged the Jap tanks single-handed with his PIAT. With his left wrist broken and wounds in the right hand and leg, Ganju Lama crawled forward and brought his weapon into action within 30 yards of the enemy tanks. He himself knocked out two tanks, the third being crippled by an anti-tank gun. He then went forward and engaged the tank crews, killing or wounding them all.

CPL (Acting Sgt.) H.V. TURNER   1st. Bn. W. YORKSHIRE REGT.

6/7 JUNE 1944   POSTHUMOUS

IN BURMA at Ningthoukhong, a strong force of Japanese attacked a platoon of about 20 men, of which Sgt. Turner was one of the Section Commanders. Three out of the four platoon L.M.G.s were destroyed, and Sgt. Turner reorganised and withdrew his dwindling party 40 yards, subsequently repelling all attacks for a period of two hours. When the enemy tried to outflank the position, Sgt. Turner left the few remaining men under his command to hold the position, and fearlessly went forward alone with all the grenades he could carry and used them with devastating effect, all the while under intense small arms and grenade fire. Sgt. Turner in all made five journeys to obtain further supplies of grenades, and it was on the sixth occasion while throwing a grenade among the enemy, that he was killed. His superb leadership and lack of thought for his own safety was undoubtedly instrumental in foiling the enemy plan. He died on the battlefield in a spirit of supreme self-sacrifice.

Naik AGANSING RAI, 2/5th ROYAL GURKHA RIFLES

JUNE 1944

NAIK AGANSING RAI' company went into attack two enemy-held positions known as "Water Piquet" and "Mortar Bluff" overlooking the Bishenpur-Silchar track in Assam. The attack faltered, but Agansing Rai led his section through withering fire across open ground to the Jap post. His Bren-gunner killed one of the machine gun crew and Agansing Rai accounted for the three who remained. The company then swept up to the position but their hold was precarious because of a 37-mm. gun pounding them from close range. Again Naik Agansing Rai took the initiative and led his section towards the gun position. When his tommy gun jammed, he seized a Bren, ran forward and killed three of the enemy. The rest were dealt with by his section and the Jap gun silenced. Later, with tommy gun in one hand and grenade in the other, he advanced on another bunker and killed the four occupants.

Subedar NETRABAHADUR THAPA, 2/5th ROYAL GURKHA RIFLES

JUNE 1944 — POSTHUMOUS

SUBEDAR NETRABAHADUR THAPA held to the last an isolated position at Water Piquet near Bishenpur, the possession of which was vital to the safety of a 14th Army base. The Japs made persistent attacks but so efficient were Netrabahadur Thapa's plans for defence and such was his example that for eight hours not a man moved from his trench and not a yard of ground was gained by the enemy. The men held on despite intense artillery fire and wave after wave of attacks by the enemy. At one time the Subedar and his runner went forward and, while Netrabahadur Thapa caused death by grenades, the runner fell to with his 'kukri'. The situation was critical and a withdrawal would have been justified, but the thought never entered the Subedar's head. After a night of grim fighting dawn found Netrabahadur Thapa killed by bullet and grenade wounds. His 'kukri' was in his hand; by his side was a dead Jap with his skull cleft.

Lt. W. B. WESTON

The Green Howards
(Attd. W. YORKS)

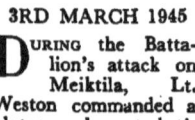

3RD MARCH 1945

DURING the Battalion's attack on Meiktila, Lt. Weston commanded a platoon whose task it was to clear through the town (a distance of 1,600 yards) with tank co-operation. The clearing of the final 800 yards commenced at 1330 hours and was to be completed by dusk, with men who were seeing active service for the first time. Opposition from bunkered positions and concrete emplacements became fanatical and each position had to be dealt with separately. With magnificent bravery Lt. Weston inspired his men

POSTHUMOUS

to superb achievements, leading them into position after position, exterminating the enemy. At 1700 hrs. within sight of the objective, the platoon was held up by a very strong bunker position. Lt. Weston directed the fire of the tanks, and led a bayonet charge into the bunker, at the entrance of which he fell wounded, but continued to fire. As he lay on the ground he withdrew the pin from a grenade and killed himself and most of the enemy inside, setting an example of heroism which can seldom have been equalled.

Naik FAZAL DIN

7/10th BALUCH REGT.

MARCH 1945

NAIK FAZAL DIN, leading his platoon against an enemy position near Meiktila in Burma, personally attacked the nearest Jap bunker and silenced it. Suddenly six of the enemy commanded by two officers appeared. The Naik, in going to the assistance of a Bren-gunner, received the sword of one of the Jap officers in his chest. As the officer withdrew the weapon, the Naik seized it and slew his opponent with it. Naik Fazal Din then killed another Jap and then,

POSTHUMOUS

running to the help of one of his sepoys, despatched a third enemy. Waving the captured sword he continued to encourage his men but when he reached platoon headquarters he collapsed, dying soon afterwards at the regimental aid post. "Such supreme devotion to duty even when fatally wounded and his presence of mind and outstanding courage has seldom been equalled and reflects the unquenchable spirit of a singularly brave and gallant N.C.O.", says the official citation.

KENNEDY PEAK

Panorama showing the Kennedy Peak—Fort White area, over which the Division fought (see page 80).

NINETEEN FORTY-TWO
Route out of Burma

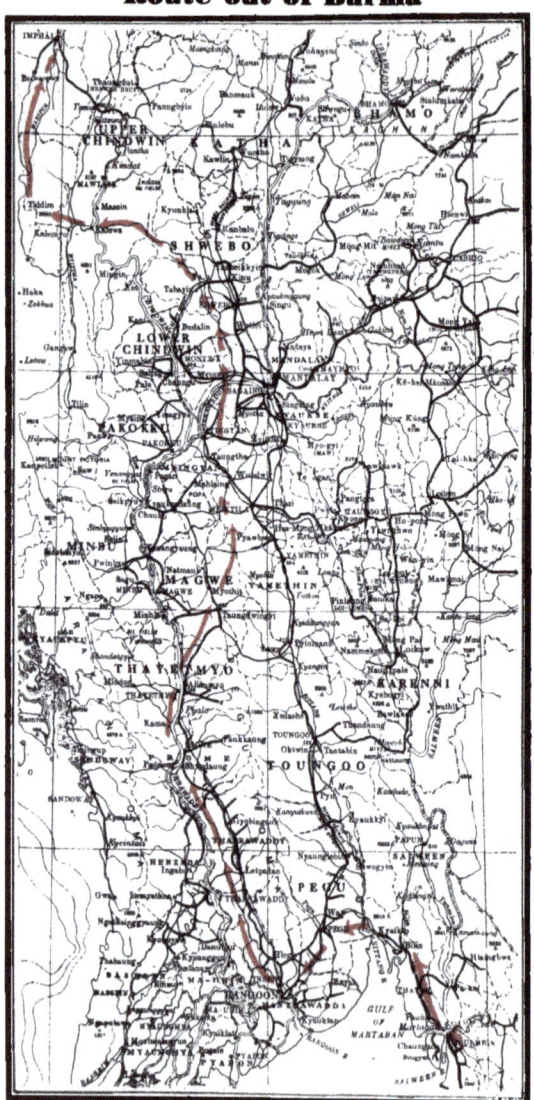

ORDER OF BATTLE.

16 Bde.	46 Bde.
1/7 G.R.	5/17 Dogr
1/9 Jat	7/10 Baluc
4/12 F.F.R.	3/7 G. R.
	1 KOYLI

18 Bde.	63 Bde.
1/3 G. R.	1/11 Sikh
1/4 G. R.	2/13 F.F. Rif.
2/5 R.G.R.	1/10 G.R

I. A.
1 Ind. Fd. Regt.
1 Ind. LAA Regt.
28 Ind. Mount Regt.
2 Ind. A/Tk Regt.

I. E.
24 Fd. Coy. (Bengal)
60 Fd. Coy. (Madras)
70 Fd. Coy. (Bengal)

Medical.
23 Fd. Amb.
37 Fd. Amb.

R. I. A. S. C.
43 A.T. Coy.
45 A.T. Coy.
47 A.T. Coy.
17 D.T.T. Coy.
46 I.B.T. Coy.

The following were under command for most of the campaign after the Battle of Sittang until the crossing of the Chindwin:

7 Armd. Bde. Group, 1 W. Yorks, 1 Cameronians, 1 Inniskilling Fusiliers, 1 Glosters, 2 D. W. R.

THE "BLACK CAT" DIVISION

Part I—The First Campaign

THE 17TH INDIAN DIVISION had the distinction of being a formation which fought against the Japanese in the withdrawal from Burma, in the Japanese offensive against India, and in the eventual liberation of Burma. It fought longer against the Japanese than any other Division and also won the largest number of Victoria Crosses of any Indian Division in the war, namely, seven. The Division rounded off its war record by occupying the very places from which the Japanese had, in January 1942, ousted it.

The "Black Cat" Division, referred to by its members proudly but justifiably as the "God's Own Division", was in action against the Japanese, apart from a few short breaks for re-organisation and training, from January 1942 until August 1945. The Division was formed in July 1941, under command of Major-General H. V. Lewis, C.B., C.I.E., D.S.O., and mobilised on 1st December, 1941. Its training in Dhond was for desert warfare and hence emphasis was laid on mobility rather than jungle tactics with which it found itself faced in a few weeks' time.

Late in December the Division was sent to Burma. Two of its brigades, 44 and 45, had already been taken away to reinforce our troops in Malaya. Thus when the Division landed in Burma, all it had was Divisional Headquarters and 46 Indian Infantry Brigade. General Lewis had fallen ill and Major-General J. G. Smyth, V.C., M.C., had taken his place. The Division went to Burma's south-eastern frontier, the Moulmein area, where 16 Indian Infantry Brigade, already deployed, was taken under command. The Division held Mergui, Tavoy, Moulmein and Kawkareik.

On January 15th the Japanese began an advance on Tavoy, having crossed the Siamese frontier by a little used track east of Myitta. For the first time in Burma our troops experienced the enemy's jungle tactics and were unable to offer serious opposition. Tavoy fell on January 19th. The garrison at Mergui was thus isolated and was therefore withdrawn by sea.

The 16th Bde. around Kawkareik was attacked on a broad front on January 19th by the Japanese 55th Division. Hostile aircraft bombed our lines of communication. A withdrawal had to be made and the Brigade fell back on Martaban by a march to the Gyaing river and thence by a river route. The Brigade lost its transport owing to a mishap to a ferry.

The Japanese then attacked Moulmein, the fort on the east bank of the Salween. With 4/12 Frontier Force Regiment, two battalions of the Burma Rifles and 12th Mountain Battery it was impossible to hold a perimeter of 12 miles against superior enemy forces. When the attack came the 4/12th F. F. R. halted the Japanese on the eastern sector. The Mountain Battery gave excellent support.

Before dawn on January 31st, however, the situation had deteriorated. The enemy was pressing the Brigade on three fronts. Moulmein was abandoned and the Brigade crossing the Salween fell back on Martaban. Martaban, Thaton and Pa-An were considered key places and each was held with a battalion or more.

The Japanese after being repulsed in a frontal attack on Martaban from Moulmein filtered across on the flanks of our garrison at Martaban. They established a block on the Martaban-Thaton road. A company of the 3/7 Gurkhas routed a body of Japanese but Martaban was no longer tenable. The 1/9 Jats and 3/7 Gurkhas marched across country to Thaton.

The 7/10 Baluch at Kuzeik was attacked by an entire regiment of Japanese on the night of February 11th/12th. The Baluchis fought magnificently. Surrounded, with their ammunition expended and wireless contact with Brigade destroyed, they fought savage hand-to-hand actions. The remnants of the battalion fought their way through the cordon and reached Duyinzeik. Between 400 and 500 Japanese were killed. One Baluch Company Commander, Captain Siri Kanth Korla, D.S.O., M.C., himself killed eleven Japanese in close fighting.

The Japanese were now in strength south of Thaton and had by-passed Duyinzeik, thereby imperilling 46 Bde. at Duyinzeik. This Brigade marched out and fell back behind 16 Bde., now holding the Bilin river bank. 48 Bde. had arrived from India and these troops came up to hold the Kyaikto-Bilin area.

Hard fighting took place in and around the village of Danyingon and on the high ground to the north-west.

Meanwhile the Japanese 33rd Division, which took heavy punishment at Kuzeik at the hands of the 7th Baluchis, had marched north and was making for the vital Sittang Bridge. In short the 17th Div. which was subjected to frontal attacks on the Bilin line was also under-threat of being encircled, the Japanese having deployed 2 Divs. to our one depleted Division. The two Brigades on the Bilin line fell back on Kyaikto, and it was decided to withdraw to the west bank of the Sittang.

The 15-mile track between Kyaikto and the Sittang was a bottle-neck. Along this route the Division made for the Sittang. Our troops and transport were frequently dive-bombed and machine-gunned. Vehicles were wrecked and the track was cratered.

Soon after Divisional Headquarters, 1/4 G. R. and H. Q. 48 Bde. had crossed the river, the Japanese attacked the bridgehead and almost reached the river, but the 4/12 F. F. R. counter-attacked and re-took the bridgehead defences. The situation was so serious that the destruction of ferry steamers and 300 sampans assembled on the west bank was ordered. Parties of Japs in the meanwhile attacked the few troops and the stationary transport in Mokpalin village.

Another attack was on our rearguard, 46 Bde. which encountered a road block seven miles short of the bridge. In a few minutes the entire Brigade was locked in close combat with an equal force of the enemy. After stiff fighting 46 Bde. broke away through the jungle and arrived in Mokpalin where intense but confused fighting was going on.

Indian engineers had worked hard to prepare the Sittang Bridge for demolition. By dawn on February 23rd it became doubtful whether the Division would be able to prevent the Japanese from breaking through and capturing the bridge. It was decided to blow up the bridge, although a large part of the Division was still on the east bank. This was done. Our troops on the east bank swam or ferried themselves across, using bamboo rafts and other devices, all the time being bombed or under machine gun fire. Many perished. Some of them eventually arrived as far north as Toungoo. Many guns and a large number of vehicles were lost.

The original plan of holding the line of the Sittang could not be carried out because of the losses the Division had suffered. A great deal of re-organisation had to be done. Some battalions were amalgamated with others. During the re-organisation Major-General D.T. ("Punch") Cowan, C.B., C.B.E., D.S.O., M.C., took over command of the Division.

The Division made a stand at Pegu but the enemy, who had crossed the Sittang in strength, was already on his way to Rangoon. 1/4 Gurkhas, The Cameronians and West Yorks assisted by the tanks of the newly arrived 7 Armoured Bde. stormed their way through a road block and our forces at Pegu reached Hlegu.

The evacuation of Rangoon had begun. 63 Bde., which had also recently arrived from India, after losing all commanding officers in an ill-fated reconnaissance, attacked another road block around Taukkyan with which the Japanese sought to bottle up the Army H. Q. and all our forces in Rangoon. An attack with infantry and tanks broke the road-block, and the Burma Army marched north along the Prome road harassed by enemy bombers. On March 8th Rangoon fell.

The task of the Division was now to assist in containing the enemy until the eastern frontiers of India could be manned, to inflict the maximum losses and conserve the maximum numbers of our own men. Already the Division, although it had suffered serious losses, had mauled two good Japanese Divisions.

The 17th moved up to Tharawaddy where stragglers arrived to swell its numbers. Clashes with the enemy occurred at Hensada and Letpadan at which latter place the Glosters ambushed a Japanese force.

Owing to a threat from the west bank of the Irrawaddy where a Japanese force was known to be moving north to Prome, the Division itself fell back on Prome which had been bombed and destroyed by the enemy.

To relieve pressure on Toungoo the 17th Division put in an offensive from Prome. Although it failed, very heavy casualties were inflicted on the enemy in a bitter action at Shwedaung where each side deployed a Brigade with full supporting arms.

In the face of sustained pressure on Prome and to forestall an enemy effort to cut the road behind the Division, the 17th withdrew from Prome being bombed heavily during its march, and fell back on Allanmyo, and moved thence to Taungdwingyi. At Kokkogwa the

48 Gurkha Brigade, holding a 'box', supported by 1 Indian Field Regiment, fought a gallant action for 2 days. This threw out the Jap time-table and allowed 1 Burma Division to escape out of the Yenangyaung trap.

Owing to the fall of the Yenangyaung oilfields and the growing threat to Pyawbwe the Division moved along a difficult track and made for Mahlaing. From there it was ordered to Kyaukse on the Meiktila-Mandalay road where it established a rearguard position.

The task of this Brigade was to protect the Chinese withdrawal on Mandalay and our final crossing of the Irrawaddy over the Ava Bridge, the only one across the river. On April 28th the Japanese bumped against the rearguard. They attacked the Gurkhas again and again but the Gurkhas did not yield ground. Over 400 Japanese were known to have been killed in the action. On the afternoon of April 29th the Brigade withdrew across the Ava Bridge without interference from an enemy who had been badly shaken. A model rearguard action, the Kyaukse battle was well planned, gallantly fought and perfectly terminated.

During the night of April 30th the Ava Bridge was blown up by Bengal Sappers and Miners.

63 Bde. thereafter went by rail to Monywa where it helped 1 Burma Division to try and dislodge an enemy force from the town. The Japanese were in greater strength than expected and our attack was halted. The Brigade along with 1 Burma Division fell back on Ye-U.

From Ye-U it was about 120 miles of very rough track through the jungle to the Chindwin. The entire Burma Army took this route to India. Magnificent engineering work, good road discipline, and staff planning made it possible for the Army to march in good order.

While the Burma Army was being ferried across the Chindwin at Shwegyin, Japanese forces landed some eight miles downstream, marched north and sought to destroy the ferry jetties. This force made a surprise attack down the defile of the Shwegyin Chaung. It took one cliff overlooking the Chaung in which our forces were assembled.

NEAR SHWEGYIN ROAD BLOCK. Sikh Gunners in action.

TWISTED STEEL and BURNING RUBBER was all that remained of abandoned Jap war material.

Elements of 17 Division were at Mutaik acting as rearguard. While the 1/9 Jats and 1/7 Gurkhas were trying to fling back the Japanese attacks, more of our infantry arrived, and guns both field and mountain, of the Indian Artillery opened fire. The Japs were driven off the cliff.

Enemy pressure increased and the jetty was rendered useless. Gen. Cowan decided to withdraw north along a hazardous path traversing razor-backed ridges to Kaing opposite Kalewa. Many vehicles, most of the guns, and much equipment were sacrificed.

After a final barrage in which they used up all ammunition, the gunners destroyed their guns and the entire force slipped away. Several hours elapsed before the tail of the column was clear of the gorge. The Japanese did not offer pursuit. They had had enough. On that May 10th over 200 Japanese bodies had been counted in the jungle.

On May 11th the rearguard crossed to Kalewa. And the rains broke. Then followed a long tiring march to Tamu. The troops arrived at Imphal, hard and thin, but still full of fight. In three months the Division had covered 1,000 miles, mostly on foot.

At the end of May '42 the Division arrived in Imphal and was re-organised. Malaria swept through the ranks as a result of the march through the Kabaw valley. It was not until October that the Division was ready again. New tactics learnt during the fighting were introduced. Detachments were sent to the Chin Hills to counter the growing threat from that direction. A motor road to Tiddim was begun.

By March the Division was on the Tiddim road, mobilised as a Light Division. There were only two Brigades, 48 and 63 but three old Battalions were retained as Divisional Troops: 1 W. Yorks as an Armd. Recce Unit, and 7/10 Baluch and 4/12 FFR as Mounted Infantry Battalions. The Division was on a jeep and pack basis.

TIDDIM and BISHENPUR

NORTH OF IMPHAL. Men of 1st Bn. W. Yorks go into action with tank support. Even the Jeep goes as far as it dares!

Water and stores arrive at one of the forward positions.

Capt. E. T. Jaffe of 1. W. Yorks on the "Walkie-talkie".

BISHENPUR. Two Jap medium tanks which were destroyed with a P.I.A.T. by Rfn. Ganju Lama, V.C., M.M.

NEAR KYAUKTO. Troops and supplies on their way into Burma.

Part II – Tiddim and Bishenpur

THE MOVE TO TIDDIM was planned to be the first phase of our advance into Burma. The Division accomplished its initial task, namely establishing a base at Tiddim, but further offensive operations had to be abandoned in view of the Japanese threat to Imphal. The Division had to go back for the defence of that beleaguered town.

ORDER OF BATTLE

Div. support Bn. — 1 W. Yorks.
Div. Recce Bns. — 7/10 Baluch.
4/12 F. F. R.

48 Bde.
1 Glosters (later, 9 Border)
2/5 R. G. R.
1/7 G. R.

ARTY.
129 Fd. Regt. R. A.
21 Ind. Mount Regt. Ind. Arty.
29 Ind. Mount Regt. Ind. Arty.
82 A/Tk Regt. R. A.

Medical.
23 Fd. Amb.
37 Fd. Amb.
50 Fd. Amb.

63 Bde.
1/3 G. R.
1/4 G. R.
1/10 G. R.

I. E.
60 Lt. Fd. (Madras).
70 Lt. Fd. (Bengal).
414 Lt. Fd. (Bengal).

R. I. A. S. C.
902-906 Jeep and A. T. Coys.

Ord.
59 Ind. Ord. Mob. Workshop Coy.
17 Ind. Rec. Coy. (Lt).

To complete the Tiddim road from M. S. 100 to M. S. 127, where the mountain side was too steep for bulldozers to work, men of 17 Light Div. were sent out on an operation called " Navvy." By the end of April, in spite of early rains and mud, the road was pushed through to the Manipur river and jeeps arrived at Tiddim.

On May 23rd the enemy attacked our advanced stockades. Although the Gurkhas fought well, the main position was overrun at No. 3 stockade. The Gurkhas fell back to the Fort White-Kennedy Peak area. 2/5 R. G. R. and 1/4 G. R. counter-attacked and retook Basha Hill in a fierce encounter. It was in this action that the Division won its first Victoria Cross, the recipient being Hav. Gaje Ghale of 2/5 R. G. R. The Gurkhas' attack stopped a Japanese offensive in the Chin Hills for a considerable period.

63 Bde. relieved 48 at Fort White and the rest of the Division moved to Shillong. The front was at Basha Hill. Throughout July and August, 63 Bde. harassed the enemy in a series of attacks, carried out in incessant rains, over roaring torrents, and through thick mud up and down thousands of feet daily. It is difficult to appreciate the strain on men and animals. In September the Japs reinforced the area and the next month they launched an attack. They overran the 1/16 Punjabis, newly put under command, but not before they suffered heavy losses. Fort White had to be abandoned. In December, 63 Bde. fought 3 battles to retake M. S. 52, where the Japs had converted the narrow pass into a veritable Corregidor with tunnels 20 feet deep in rock. The position was never taken.

In January the enemy sent out two columns, one of which ran into the 7/10 Baluch and was decimated. The other column established posts along the Falam road.

Sappers had made the road to Kennedy Peak fit for 3 tonners. Medium guns arrived at Kennedy Peak. The next few weeks were spent in an attack on M. S. 52 which was encircled slowly. A minefield 3 miles long was laid at night in thick jungle.

To the west, 63 Bde. had met with success in its attack on Lophei Spur where the enemy garrison was hemmed in with barbed wire. Faced with a threat of starvation, the Japanese escaped through a gap in the wire with 50% casualties.

The Division was now spread out over a frontage of 80 miles.

On March 6th the enemy offensive on Imphal-Kohima began. The Japanese cut the Tiddim road at M. S. 100. Tonzang was threatened. The Division decided to dig in, but orders were received for a move to Imphal which was then under siege.

On March 14th the withdrawal began. Within 27 hours, 16,000 troops on foot, 2,500 vehicles and 3,500 animals had been withdrawn from positions covering 20 miles within a 15-mile radius of Tiddim. The advance into Burma was abandoned and the move back to protect Imphal began.

The Japs in their usual manner by-passed our troops and cut the road behind them at M. S. 132 near Tuitim village. 63 Bde. with air and artillery support cleared the block and wiped out more than half the enemy force.

Protected then by a chain of piquets which neutralized the Jap flank position, the Division moved from M. S. 142 to 110, during which time frequent attacks by the enemy of Bn. strength with tanks were going in on the Tuitum saddle, all of which however were beaten off by the garrison of 1½ Coys. 1/10 G. R. Five tanks were simultaneously destroyed in one night and the crews committed suicide. The enemy had blocked the road between M. S. 110-100 and a Brigade of 23 Indian Division from the other side had been attacking the block which they ultimately cleared after heavy fighting. 48 Bde. attacked the high ground overlooking M. S. 110. The Sappers made mule paths while the battle raged about them. The high ground was taken. Another enemy force established at M. S. 105 was also driven off.

On March 26th the Division moved again. Another attack was made by the "Black Cats" to clear the stretch

View across Meiktila Lake from Meiktila Garrison position, held by Maj.-Gen. Kasuya and 3,200 men.

M. S. 102 to 100 and then they moved to M. S. 82. With the help of 7 Cavalry which had come under command, the Division soon re-opened the road to Imphal.

The Division went straight into the Imphal battle, its task being the protection of the airfield which was threatened.

During the next month a Regt. of Jap. 15 Div., committed to the capture of the airfield, launched continuous attacks against 63 Bde. holding Sengmai. Two Jap Bns. were decimated in the process.

On April 14th the Division with 33 Bde. of 20 Div. under command took over the defence of the Tiddim road. For the success of their plan the Japanese had to capture Bishenpur. This they never did.

Towards the end of April, 33 (Japanese) Division attacked Bishenpur. They attacked against M. S. 21 and infiltrated between two battalion positions. But the road was re-opened and by May 20th the area was cleared. Over 600 casualties were inflicted on the Japanese 215 Regiment.

One Brigade of 17 Division (63 Bde.) early in May 1944 attacked the village of Postangbam and cleared it. Over 300 casualties were inflicted. Simultaneously 48 Bde. carried out a 30-mile "hook" and put a road block behind the Japanese at M. S. 40. For 7 days Jap reinforcing Bns. tried to break this. Only when because maintenance became too difficult was the Bde. withdrawn through the centre of the Jap positions. There was more fighting, some of which was bitter, but the 17th was now in glorious form. Only 200 of the 2,700 Japs who took part in the Bishenpur operation escaped slaughter.

The next plan was to clear the road to Tiddim. Many villages were retaken. But the Jap about this time began a last and fiercer battle for Imphal. Fighting was general and the Division accomplished a great deal by counter-attacks and well-planned defence. At Ningthoukhong, Rfn. Ganju Lama, M.M., of 1/7 G. R. and Cpl. H. V. Turner, W. Yorks, won the Victoria Cross, Cpl. Turner posthumously.

The 2/5 R. G. R. was in action on the Bishenpur-Silchar track. Naik Agansing Rai and Subedar Netrabahadur Thapa won the Victoria Cross, the latter posthumously, in one action. The Division thus won four Victoria Crosses in the Imphal fighting.

The Japanese 33 Division, disease-ridden and starving, began to fall back and the 17th set off in pursuit. On July 19th it was withdrawn to Imphal and moved thence to Ranchi. It is estimated that 33 Division reinforced to 12 Bns. was decimated in these operations.

After training and re-equipping in December 1944 the Division was back in Imphal.

ORDER OF BATTLE
December 1944—August 1945

Div. Recce. Bn. — 6 Rajput.
Defence — 6 Jat (after Meiktila, 1. E. Yorks).
M. G. Bn. — 9 F. F. Rif.

48 Bde.	63 Bde.	99 Bde.
1 W. Yorks.	9 Border.	6/15 Punjab.
4 F. F. R.	7 Baluch.	1 Sikh L. I.
1/7 G. R.	1/10 G. R.	1/3 G. R.

ARTY.	I. E.
129 Fd. Regt. R. A.	60 Coy. (Madras).
1 Ind. Fd. Regt.	70 Coy. (Bengal).
21 Ind. Mtn. Regt.	Tehri Garhwal Coy.
82 A/Tk. Regt. R. A.	414 Ind. Fd. Park (Bengal).
R. I. A. S. C.	**Medical.**
902 G. T. Coy.	23 Fd. Amb.
906 G. T. Coy.	37 ,, ,,
50 Gwalior Pony Coy.	50 ,, ,,
42 A. T. Coy.	22 Hyg. Sec.
I. E. M. E.	**Ord.**
1, 59, 123 Workshop	117 Ordnance Fd. Pk.
17 Rec.	2 Workshop Coys

255 Tk. Bde. (5 Probyn's Horse, 9 Royal Deccan Horse)
16 L. Cavalry, 247 Medium Bty. 189 H. A. A. Bty.
Squadron of 11 P. A. V. O. Cavalry
250 L. A. A. Bty. 57 Coy. D. Force.

RETURN to BURMA.

KYAUKSE. Great work done by Sappers in rebuilding blown bridges. Lorries down-stream ford river.

Gen. Cowan (right) discusses advance beyond Taungtha with Brig. Dimoline, C.R.A. (left) and Wing Commander R.G.K. Thompson.

DRIVE ON SEYWA. 3" Mortar detachment of 12 F. F. Regt. in support of Infantry.

SEYWA. Men of the 12 F. F. Regt. charge on the burning remnants of Seywa during the drive on Meiktila.

MEIKTILA ADVANCE. Armoured car on patrol moves off in the direction of burning Meiktila.

Sappers search for mines on the road to Meiktila.

THE ROAD TO MEIKTILA. Sappers fill in crater to facilitate the advance.

JEEP being unloaded by Gurkhas from a Dakota on captured Jap airfield.

TINDAW. Jap defences at YEWE village S. E. Meiktila are blasted out of existence by tanks firing at point-blank range.

PYAWBWE. 37 m.m. gun of Indian Mountain Regiment pounds the Jap by night as well as by day.

PYAWBWE. Troops of 1st Sikh L. I. attack village 3 miles east of Pyawbwe through thick scrub.

PYAWBWE. Smoke screen covers men of the Sikh Light Infantry during the attack 3 miles east of Pyawbwe.

PEGU. British Troops "mopping up" in burning PEGU.

BEYOND PEGU. Convoys ford river during drive on Rangoon.

PYINBONGYI, 70 miles from Rangoon blazes as Bren gunners and tanks of the Royal Deccan Horse watch for bolting Japs.

TANKS and VEHICLES advance during the attack on Pyinbongyi.

HLEGU. The climax to a bitter campaign. Gurkhas advance to the last barrier before Rangoon.

HLEGU. Crossing the chaung beneath a blown bridge.

HLEGU. Pathans of the 9th F. F. Rifles give covering fire to troops during the river crossing.

NINETEEN FORTY-FIVE
Route back into Burma.

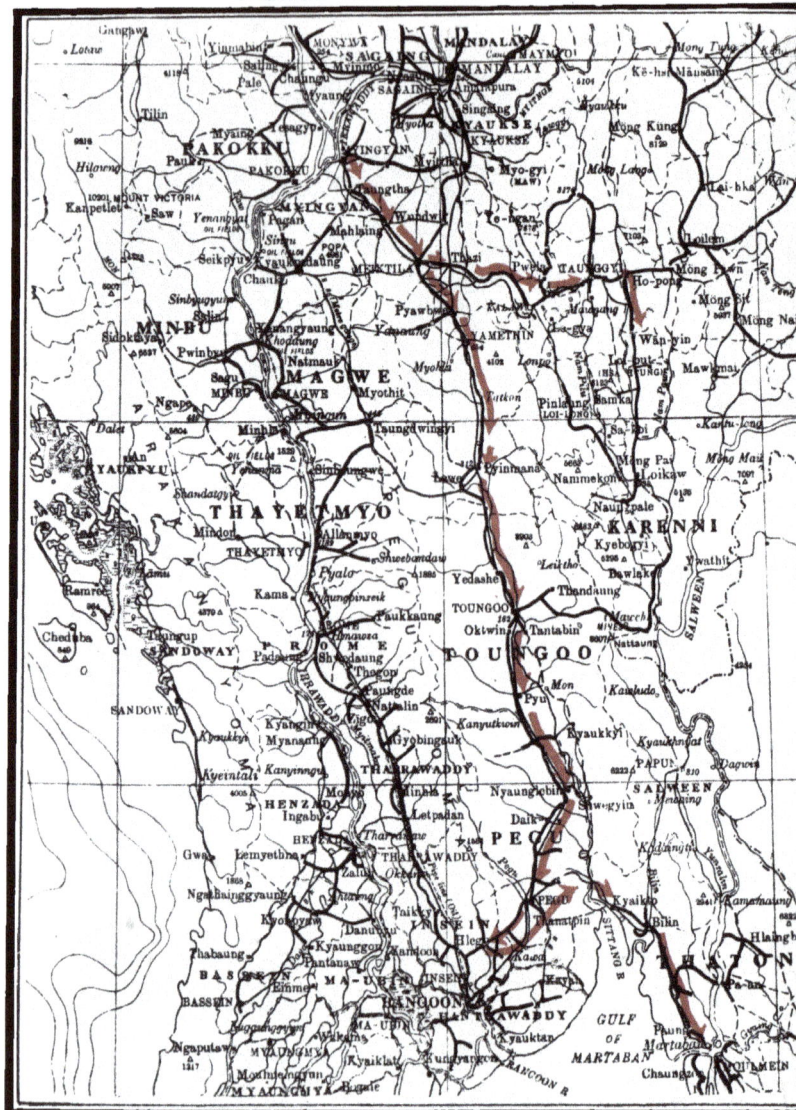

Part III—Return to Burma

IN THE 17TH DIVISION'S CAMPAIGN against the Japanese it had lost the first round on points and had drawn the second. The third round saw the Division gloriously triumphant. In this phase the "Black Cats" avenged all previous reverses. The Division took Meiktila and held it against heavy counter-attacks. Around Meiktila the men of the 17th fought successful battles which made the subsequent liberation of Rangoon a comparatively easy task.

The Army plan was for a mechanised column to drive through the lines of communication of the enemy who was fighting a defensive battle around Mandalay. Meiktila, an important road junction in Central Burma, was the objective.

The Division, doing another lightning change and becoming a motorised division in eight days, drove secretly down the Gangaw valley in the wake of the 7th Indian Division which was to make the crossing of the Irrawaddy at Nyaungu, near Pagan, the ancient capital of Burma.

By Feb. 18th the 17th with 255 Indian Armoured Brigade under command was across the river and had started on its drive to Meiktila. This town was 82 miles away and such a long line of communication could not be maintained through hostile territory. Hence the Division sealed off its rear as it proceeded and subsisted on supplies dropped from aircraft.

Armoured cars in front, then tanks and infantry, more infantry, then the 3,000 vehicles of the column and finally a rearguard of infantry and tanks—such was the order of march. Every night the Division went into harbour behind a perimeter, bristling with weapons which the enemy in vain tried to breach.

The column dashed into Ngathayauk, 16 miles from Nyaungu and then split into two. One took the Sektein-Welaung road, the other the Kamye road. Both forces crushed resistance as they went along. Water was the chief difficulty in this arid tract of Central Burma.

The two forces converged on Taungtha which fell easily. In fact the enemy garrison was slaughtered almost to a man, the 7/10 Baluch Regt. doing most of the killing.

From Taungtha the Division advanced to Thabutkin and captured an airfield. The third Brigade of the Division (99) was flown in from Imphal.

After brushing aside a road block at M. S. 8½, the Division arrived on the outskirts of Meiktila. This town, as events proved, had a garrison of 3,200 Japanese. General Cowan blocked all roads leading into Meiktila and put in a three-pronged attack on the town. Fighting was savage. The Japanese asked for no quarter; every one of them had to be slain before resistance ceased. On the fourth day of the battle Meiktila was in our hands. In the action Nk. Fazal Din of 7th Baluch Regt. and Lieut. W. B. Weston of the West Yorks both posthumously won the Victoria Cross.

Immediately the town was divided into sectors and each sector was wired round and made ready for siege. It was just as well, because the enemy reacted strongly to this cutting of his lines of communication. The Japanese concentrated three Divisions against Meiktila from all directions and with strong artillery and tank support sought to retake the town. They succeeded in penetrating to the airfield from which, however, they were driven off. Aircraft of the R.A.F., R.I.A.F. and U.S.A.A.F. gave most valuable help to the Division.

Columns, usually of Brigade strength (less one Bn. left to guard the perimeter) and supported by a Regt. of Tanks and all the Div. Arty., carried out sweeps —lasting 48 hours—with the intention of catching the enemy unprepared before they had had time to formulate plans of attack, subsequent to later concentration. These tactics were very effective, and the enemy, in spite of bitter fighting, were destroyed piecemeal. The columns always had two days' rest, bathing in the lake, secure behind their wire, before the next sortie. Time and again the Japs counter-attacked at night, always abortively. In one night attack against a sector held by 1/7 G. R. and 4/12 F. F. R. the enemy lost 281 men. The dead lay thick in front of the wire fence.

For one month the Division stayed in Meiktila. It had under command an extra brigade (9 Bde. of 5 Division), which had been flown in. With the failure of their attacks on Meiktila, resulting in almost the complete destruction of three already weak Divisions the Japanese front in Burma collapsed and a general withdrawal, developing into a rout, began.

On March 30th, therefore, the Division, leaving a garrison in Meiktila, set out on its march to Rangoon. Pyawbwe was the immediate objective.

Infantry battalions were vying with one another to create records in casualties inflicted on the enemy. The Sikh Light Infantry one day ran into an ambush and the next day avenged their reverse with a bayonet charge which became the talk of the 14th Army.

There was strong resistance at Yindaw but the town was by-passed. Then General Cowan sent out three columns which converged on Pyawbwe. Here again over 1,000 Japanese were killed. Pyawbwe fell on April 10th.

5 Indian Division now took the lead. On April 25th, however, the 17th going through 5 Division advanced south of Toungoo.

The Japanese were in retreat and the 17th was in full cry. There was fighting at Nyaunglebin and at

Payagalo, and then Pegu was captured, the Japs losing the remainder of their guns. Rangoon had been evacuated and the Japanese forces—military and civilian—were streaming across the Sittang.

The advance on Hlegu was carried out by two columns. The rains had begun prematurely and the resultant mud added to the difficulties. On the point of reaching its goal the Division faced a bitter disappointment. The bridge at Hlegu had been destroyed. Before a new bridge could be built by Sappers, Rangoon had been taken by troops of 26th Indian Division coming in from the sea.

In this operation the Division had done about 725 miles (Imphal to Hlegu) in under three months. It accounted for 10,263 enemy killed, 167 captured, 212 guns and 15 tanks.

Although Rangoon had fallen and the Rangoon-Mandalay road was in our hands, a large number of Japanese still remained and fought in south western Burma. They assembled in the Pegu Yomas where they faced starvation or annihilation. They decided to break out east, try and force their way through our long tenuous lines and go across the Sittang river to eastern Burma which was still enemy-held.

The trapped enemy forces made their attempt to break out in the third week of July. The 17th Division which was strung out over 75 miles of country along the Mandalay road, had been reinforced with units from other Divisions. Floods and the mud made deployment difficult, but the Japanese conveniently ran into them. The slaughter was incredible. A lack of co-ordination in the Japanese attack made its failure inevitable. The final enemy casualty figures were: Killed 5,057; prisoners 561. The Division itself suffered less than 250 casualties. Thus the second battle of the Sittang saw the tables neatly turned.

One Brigade of the Division meanwhile was driving the enemy back in the Southern Shan States. This force reached Taunggyi.

On August 23rd the Japanese made contact with the 17th for surrender negotiations. That was the end of the fighting history of one of the most remarkable Infantry Divisions which fought during the late war.

*　　　　　*　　　　　*

DECORATIONS AND AWARDS

	Units of Div.	Units under Cmd.	Total
V.C.	7	..	
C.B.	1	..	1
C.B.E.	2	..	2
I.O.M.	26	1	27
D.S.O.	20	2	22
Bar to D.S.O.	8	..	8
O.B.E.	6	..	6
I.D.S.M.	82	2	84
Bar to I.D.S.M.	1	..	1
O.B.I.	4	..	4
M.B.E.	17	..	17
M.C.	133	23	156
Bar to M.C.	3	1	4
M.M.	220	36	256
Bar to M.M.	3	..	3
D.C.M.	7	1	8
B.E.M.	2	..	2
B.G.M.	1	5	6
Russian decorations.	2	..	2
Mention in despatches.	396	20	416

CASUALTIES
(Less JAN '42 TO MAY '42)

Killed			Wounded			Missing		
Officers	VCOs	ORs	Officers	VCOs	ORs	Officers	VCOs	ORs
106	46	1880	189	162	6704	2	1	372

SURRENDER!

ABYA. Major Wako Lisanori of Jap 28th Army hands his sword to Lt.-Col. O. N. Smyth, Comd., 1/10th Gurkha Rifles.

MOKPALIN. *Jap Ps. O. W. aboard a landing craft in which they crossed the Sittang River.*

MOULMEIN. *Lt.-Gen. Honda, C-in-C, Jap 33rd Army, hands over his sword to Maj.-Gen. Crowther.*

SYMBOL of VICTORY
Union Jack being hoisted again over Mokpalin on the east bank of the Sittang.

BADGES OF CORPS AND UNITS WHICH SERVED WITH THE DIVISION
Indian Army—(Continued).

INDIAN DIVISIONS WON A FINE REPUTATION IN WORLD WAR TWO

Field Marshal Auchinleck, Commander-in-Chief of the British Indian Army from 1942, asserted that the British *"couldn't have come through both wars (World War I and II) if they hadn't had the British Indian Army"*. British Prime Minister Winston Churchill also paid tribute to *"the unsurpassed bravery of Indian soldiers and officers"*.

Between 1945 and 1947, the Director of Public Relations, War Department, Government of India, published a series of short publications covering the individual histories of the WWII Indian Divisions. They followed a consistent format, having between 44 and 48 pages within illustrated soft card covers. They have an average of 50 monochrome photographic illustrations, and each has a full colour centrespread depicting a scene from the Division's wartime operations (drawn by official war artists). They were printed at various presses in Bombay and New Delhi, and each contains at least one map.

As condensed histories they are useful – particularly those which relate to Divisions for which no other record was ever produced.

The British Indian Army during World War II began the war, in 1939, numbering just under 200,000 men. By the end of the war, it had become the largest volunteer army in history, rising to over 2.5 million men in August 1945. Serving in divisions of infantry, armour and a fledgling airborne force, they fought on three continents: in Africa, Europe and Asia.

This Army fought in Ethiopia against the Italian Army, in Egypt, Libya, Tunisia and Algeria against both the Italian and German Army and, after the Italian surrender, against the German Army in Italy. However, the bulk of the British Indian Army was committed to fighting the Japanese Army, first during the British defeats in Malaya and the retreat from Burma to the Indian border; later, after resting and refitting for the victorious advance back into Burma, as part of the largest British Empire army ever formed. These campaigns cost the lives of over 87,000 Indian service- men, while another 34,354 were wounded, and 67,340 became prisoners of war. Their valour was recognised with the award of some 4,000 decorations, and 18 members of the British Indian Army were awarded the Victoria Cross or the George Cross.

RED EAGLES
The Story of the 4th Indian Division
9781474537520

During the Second World War, the 4th Indian Division was in the vanguard of nine campaigns in the Mediterranean theatre, Egypt, Eritrea, Syria, Tunisia, Italy and Greece. The 4th Division captured 150,000 prisoners and suffered 25,000 casualties, more than the strength of a whole division. It won over 1,000 honours and awards, which included four Victoria Crosses and three George Crosses. Field Marshal Lord Wavell wrote: "The fame of this Division will surely go down as one of the greatest fighting formations in military history."

THE FIGHTING FIFTH
History of the 5th Indian Division
9781474537513

As described in much greater detail in Anthony Brett James's book 'The Ball of Fire', the division saw active service in East Africa, North Africa and Burma.

GOLDEN ARROW
The Story of the 7th Indian Division
9781474537506

The role of this division is also duplicated by a much larger work: the book by Brig. M. R. Roberts. However, this booklet gives a good account of Kohima and Imphal and the crossing of the Irrawaddy. In 1945, the division was flown into Siam, so becoming the first Allied formation to re-enter South East Asia.

ONE MORE RIVER
The Story of the 8th Indian Division
Biferno, Trigno, Sangro, Moro, Rapido, Arno, Senio, Santerno, Po, Adige

9781474537490

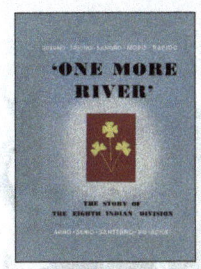

The 8th Indian Division started its overseas service in the Middle East in the garrisoning of Iraq and then the invasion of Persia to secure the oil fields of the area for the Allies, before moving to Italy in 1943. Landing at Taranto, it pushed up the length of the peninsula in a series of major battles: breaking the Sangro Line, forcing the Rapido and turning the defences at Cassino, breaking the stubborn German resistance at Monte Grande and, finally, forcing the Po River. It won four VCs, 26 DSOs and 149 MCs along the way. During the war the 8th Indian Division sustained casualties totalling 2,012 dead, 8,189 wounded and 749 missing.

BLACK CAT DIVISION
17th Indian Division

9781474537483

This formation was committed to Burma from the early days when the British were in full flight from the invading Japanese. It remained in Burma right through to the end, when the starving remnants of the Japanese Army were making their own desperate retreat.

TIGER HEAD
The Story of the 26th Indian Division
Arakan, Ragoon

9781474537452

This is a history of the division said later by the Japanese to have been the opponent which they most feared. The 26th held the Allied monsoon line in the Arakan during two such seasons, repulsing every attack launched against it. Later it made a series of leap-frog landings down the coast to clinch the issue in the Arakan. It was the first division to enter Ragoon, invading the city from the sea.

A HAPPY FAMILY
The Story of the Twentieth Indian Division, April 1942-August 1945

9781474537476

One of the few Indian divisions in the 14th Army trained specifically for the war in Burma. Raised in Bangalore in 1942, it commenced active operations in late 1943 and served from Imphal through to the end. It established the 14th Army's first brigade-head across the Chindwin and its second such brigade-head across the Irrawaddy. Its final task was to round up the Japanese in French Indochina.

THE TWENTY THIRD INDIAN DIVISION
"The Fighting Cock Division"
Burma, Malaya, Java

9781474537469

The Fighting Cock Division is well recorded in the book by Doulton. This book gives coverage of the heavy fighting at the Kohima Battle, the capture of Tamu, the reoccupation of Malaya in August 1945, and then its strange role on the island of Java – concurrently disarming the Japanese garrison, fighting the insurgent Indonesian nationalists, and caring for 65,000 former internees pending the arrival of a new Dutch administration.

TEHERAN TO TRIESTE
The Story Of The Tenth Indian Division

9781783317028

This History deals with the 10th Indian Div's exploits in Iraq (under Maj Gen "Bill" Slim) its role in the Libyan battles leading up to El Alamein, the following two years of garrison duties in Cyprus and Syria, and finally, its fighting services in the Italian campaign (from Ortona onwards).

THE STORY OF THE 25th INDIAN DIVSION
The Arakan Campaign
9781783317585

Formed in Southern India in August 1942 for defence of that area in case of Japanese invasion, the "Ace of Spades" Division had its baptism of fire in Arakan in February 1944. It served throughout the remainder of that campaign the climax being the battle of Tamandu. Its victorious fight for the Kangaw roadblock was considered by many to have been the fiercest battle of the entire Burma war, while its liberation of Akyab was the first convincing proof to the rest of the world that the tide had turned against the Japanese.

DAGGER DIVISION
The Story Of The 19th Indian Division
9781783317035

Raised in the late 1941, the 19th was the first "standard" Indian Division. Its troops were the first to breach the Japanese defence line in Burma and to raise the flag at Fort Dufferin. It crossed the Chindwin in November 1944, driving on to Mandalay and Ragoon during seven months of continuous fighting. The 19th's exploits are graphically described also in John Masters' personal memoir, *The Road Past Mandalay*.

www.ingramcontent.com/pod-product-compliance
Lightning Source LLC
Chambersburg PA
CBHW041928090426
42743CB00021B/3478